THINGS MY SPONSORS TAUGHT ME

PAUL H.

HAZELDEN INFORMATION AND EDUCATIONAL SERVICES is a division of the Hazelden Foundation, a not-for-profit organization. Since 1949, Hazelden has been a leader in promoting the dignity and treatment of people afflicted with the disease of chemical dependency.

The mission of the foundation is to improve the quality of life for individuals, families, and communities by providing a national continuum of information, education, and recovery services that are widely accessible; to advance the field through research and training; and to improve our quality and effectiveness through continuous improvement and innovation.

Stemming from that, the mission of this division is to provide quality information and support to people wherever they may be in their personal journey—from education and early intervention, through treatment and recovery, to personal and spiritual growth.

Although our treatment programs do not necessarily use everything Hazelden publishes, our bibliotherapeutic materials support our mission and the Twelve Step philosophy upon which it is based. We encourage your comments and feedback.

The headquarters of the Hazelden Foundation are in Center City, Minnesota. Additional treatment facilities are located in Chicago, Illinois; New York, New York; Plymouth, Minnesota; St. Paul, Minnesota; and West Palm Beach, Florida. At these sites, we provide a continuum of care for men and women of all ages. Our Plymouth facility is designed specifically for youth and families.

For more information on Hazelden, please call **1-800-257-7800**. Or you may access our World Wide Web site on the Internet at **http://www.hazelden.org**.

THINGS MY SPONSORS TAUGHT ME

PAUL H.

HAZELDEN®

First published August, 1987.

ISBN: 0-89486-444-0

Printed in the United States of America.

CONTENTS

INTRODUCTION

On a rainy Tuesday night in May, about fifteen years ago, I met two men who changed — and saved — my life. Some might say it was an incredible stroke of fortune that I met them. Those of us in Alcoholics Anonymous recognize that, as these two men told me, "Coincidence is when God chooses to remain anonymous!"

The realistic, honest, and straightforward way they had of making sense out of the complex business of recovery was like a splash of cold water in my face — refreshing, jarring, but always to the point and always helpful. Their wisdom became integral to my recovery; it is still helping others, since I quote my first sponsors all the time. In fact, this book consists of quotes from my first sponsors, and a little commentary on their teachings. It seems right and proper to pass along their teachings to others who seek the help of the fellowship of A.A. and its self-help offspring, such as Narcotics Anonymous.

With gratitude and strong affection, this is dedicated to Harve F. and Bob M. "Thanks, guys!" seems tame, but you know I mean it as much as anything I've ever said in my life.

ABOUT ALCOHOLICS ANONYMOUS

On the Purpose of A.A.

> *A.A. is for people who don't want to drink any-
> more. It's not for people who want to control it or
> learn to hold it better, but for those who just don't
> want to drink* at all *anymore.*

There are several things to notice in this quotation. First,
it says nothing about alcoholics or alcoholism. I am an "alcoholic," but A.A. wouldn't refuse me if the word was too much
for me to say. Second, A.A. is not for those who wish to cut
down, change brands, or drink like ladies or gentlemen. A.A.
is for those who want to stop. A final note is about the word
"want." Millions of alcoholics and alcohol abusers *need* to
stop, but only those who *want* to stop will be helped by A.A.

On Rules and A.A.

> *There are no "musts" in A.A., but there are a
> lot of "you darned well betters."*

All the literature and traditions of the fellowship of A.A.
are gentle, nonjudgmental, and persuasive. There aren't any
musts. There are no "Thou shalt nots" in the A.A. Big Book*

---

*The Big Book is *Alcoholics Anonymous,* published by A.A. World
Services, Inc. New York, NY. Available through Hazelden Educational
Materials, order no. 2020.

3

or the Twelve and Twelve.** A.A. members and A.A. groups are free to do as they wish. A.A., which is more than 50 years old, is a distillation of the experiences, good and bad, of millions of people. So when the wisdom of A.A. or the group conscience recommends not doing something or not going somewhere, you are well advised not to do it or not to go there. It is worthwhile listening to the fellowship, because there is no problem, no situation, and no feeling you may experience that many people before you haven't already experienced and survived sober. "Stick with the winners" remains very good advice, even if what the winners do doesn't quite seem to be your cup of tea at the moment.

On the Nature of A.A.

This is a "Save-Your-Ass" program, not a "Save-Your-Soul" program; we're concerned with the here-and-now, not the Hereafter.

A.A. does not put down alcoholics. After all, we are dealing with people just like ourselves. Programs traditionally associated with a more moralistic view toward alcoholism — often with a specifically religious orientation — emphasize reformation of a sinner for the soul's good. The alcoholic in crisis has a lousy self-image, and being prayed over usually accentuates this.

A.A. — being formed by, of, and for alcoholics — has a different view of things. We aren't against religion; we merely recognize that religion, of itself, is not a part of recovery.

We must feel this way or else an alcoholic who lacks religion must either become religious or be rejected. We alcoholics know rejection; we aren't going to practice it on our own kind.

**The Twelve and Twelve is *Twelve Steps and Twelve Traditions,* published by A.A. World Services, Inc. New York, NY. Available through Hazelden Educational Materials, order no. 2080.

4

On Alternatives to A.A. for the Alcoholic

*Death if you're lucky, insanity if you're not —
take your pick.*

To some people, this must seem heartless. Actually, it is heartfelt, because it is nothing less than the simple truth. In most cases, an alcoholic has only three alternatives: death, insanity, or abstinence. There are some who have learned to live without alcohol and without the fellowship of A.A. There are reputed to be a few who have learned how to go back to "normal drinking." There aren't, however, many in either category. As my sponsors said, "Before you go out to try it alone, consider the consequences if you gamble that you can make it on your own and find out you're wrong!"

A.A. treats alcoholism as a progressive, irreversible, and terminal disease. Therefore, in A.A.'s way of thinking, the alcoholic can never return to social drinking, because the alcoholic can recover from alcoholism but cannot be cured.

ABOUT JOINING
ALCOHOLICS ANONYMOUS:
WHY AND HOW

On Reasons for Joining A.A.

People who come to A.A. for anyone but themselves are trying to swim with concrete flippers — it can be done, but it's a whole lot more difficult than it needs to be.

Again and again, we see people who have come to A.A. because of their wives, husbands, bosses, judges, and so on. Unless these folks come to terms with their denial and compliance (for example, "I'll agree to anything, if you'll only shut up!"), they have less than average chances of success. If I'm not in A.A. to save my own fanny, I will most likely not get better.

I had a friend who sobered up the first time for her job; when she retired, she got drunk. She sobered up again, this time for her husband. But he died. And then so did she.

On Giving A.A. a Try

Try us for 90 days; if you're not satisfied, we'll refund all your miseries.

I didn't believe them when they told me this. I was an "almost" alcoholic — almost divorced, almost fired, almost jailed, and almost killed. When I came to the program, life was just about intolerable. To an alcoholic, "intolerable" means "I'm having thoughts of suicide." The A.A. people said, "Go to 90 meetings in 90 days." Because one of them was nearly always with me — either on the phone, at my doorstep, or riding with me on the commuter train — I did go to 90 meetings in 90 days.

After spending only 90 days in the fellowship of A.A., my life was a mess — it still is! With seven children, grandchildren, and assorted animals, my wife and I live in a soap opera. To tell the truth, we probably prefer it that way. But thoughts of suicide are gone. Some of the wounds in my family are healing. I'm acting like normal people do, getting up and going to work and even doing a good job. I sleep well at night. I eat like a pig, and, at the same time, I've lost around 30 pounds. My miseries have pretty much gone away — nothing dramatic, they've just gone away. And they haven't been back, either!

On Joining and Quitting A.A.

You join A.A. by going to meetings; you quit by taking a drink.

My first sponsors were hard-noses. They did not fool around with their recovery programs. One of the A.A. slogans they didn't invent but would have if someone else hadn't beat them to it is: "**Keep it simple, stupid**," also known as the **KISS** system. If you're attending A.A. meetings and you're still drinking, you haven't joined yet. You quit A.A. when you pick up the glass because A.A. members don't drink. Not at all. Simple, isn't it?

You may be thinking that you're an alcoholic who has learned to drink socially. My first sponsors told me about a practice in many A.A. clubhouses of having an empty picture frame on the wall, inscribed, "Reserved for the first A.A. member to successfully return to social drinking." No one has ever asked to have his or her picture hung in that frame!

On Insurance

> *You go to A.A. meetings for the same reasons*
> *you have insurance, for protection when you need*
> *it — and you would be in a hell of a place with-*
> *out it.*

By this reasoning, A.A. meetings may be seen as premium payments. There are times when we have nothing within ourselves to withstand the temptation to drink. That's why we have the insurance policy we acquire when we belong to A.A. and go to meetings regularly. I can remember my sponsors telling me that you can tell an A.A. member by his wallet or her purse full of phone numbers. Now that my own wallet has burst from being overstuffed with phone numbers, I understand the concept of A.A. as insurance.

The temptations we face as recovering alcoholics are often quite easy to overcome. But we never know when a temptation will come along that's too much for us to handle alone. The cost of not being able to handle a temptation may be too high. A.A.'s position is that we can't afford to let our God-given insurance lapse, because we never know if we'll receive the grace period to reinstate it. As my sponsors said, "We all have another drunk left in us; we don't know whether we have another recovery in us."

On Having an A.A. "Birthday"

> *Congratulations, but you really ought to know*
> *that the Nth year is the dangerous one.*

The "Nth year" is this year. The message is that the dangerous year of sobriety is the present. Years past are either successful or otherwise, and years to come aren't here yet. There is a rather somber aspect to this quote, or at least it seemed so to me when I first heard it. My sponsor was having a meeting at his house in observation of his eleventh A.A. birthday. His sponsor, who at the time was 23 years sober,

9

made the quote. I had less than a year of sobriety at the time, and it bothered me to think that the potential for relapse would exist as long as 23 years.

From my present vantage point, with about fifteen years under my belt, it is sobering to realize that my recovery is an ongoing process that can be interrupted anytime I pick up a drink, no matter how many years I may have with the A.A. program. I don't worry about this a lot, but I do spend some time on each of my A.A. birthdays remembering that the key word for me is "recovering," not "recovered."

ABOUT ALCOHOLICS ANONYMOUS MEETINGS: WHEN AND HOW MANY

On Going to Meetings (#1)

Nobody ever got drunk from going to A.A. meetings.

Obviously, the first benefit of going to A.A. meetings is that they keep one from drinking — at least for the period during the meeting. What my sponsors meant by their remark, I think, is more subtle. The act of going to an A.A. meeting is a form of commitment to A.A. and has a time value beyond the actual evening of the meeting. Even more than a time value, this commitment to A.A. is a commitment to what A.A. stands for, which is not drinking. That's why the common response to many alcoholics' complaints is, "Go to a meeting!"

Meetings have a wonderful therapeutic value. The day could be stormy, full of doubts and frustrated emotions, but going to a meeting helps to hasten serenity. Do you have a problem with your recovery program? Take it to a meeting and let the group conscience work on it for a while, and you'll be surprised and helped by the results.

If you're in doubt about whether you should go to a meeting, resolve the question on the side of caution, and go. At least 99.9 percent of the time, it's the right decision.

On Going to Meetings (#2)

For an alcoholic, there is nothing *more pressing than a meeting.*

This was spoken to a new recruit who had exclaimed, "But Tuesday is bowling night!" Especially for alcoholics who are newly sober through A.A., sobriety is a fragile thing in the early days, and to let anything have a higher place than one's A.A. meetings is to risk it all.

A.A. meetings are more important than any bowling league, television show, baseball game, or whatever. One can always bowl earlier or later or in another league. One may not have another chance at sobriety, and the alternative simply doesn't bear thinking about.

On Finding the Necessary Number of Meetings (#1)

How many days per week did you drink? That's a good place to start.

Regular A.A. attendance replaces the social part of the drinking scene and, thus, assumes an importance of its own. The value of doing something else to avoid the drinking scene is difficult to overstate. So, as my sponsors reasoned, if you went to taverns five nights per week, you'd better go to A.A. meetings five nights per week, at least at first.

Another way to look at this advice is to realize one should make as determined an effort at sobriety as one earlier made at drinking. Therefore, the five nights per week drinking commitment is replaced by a five nights per week A.A. commitment.

The wisdom behind the A.A. message of 90 meetings in 90 days should not be ignored. After my "90 in 90," I settled into a routine of going to a certain number of meetings per week that I continued for almost three years. Then I cut back a meeting or so, but not until then. I'm still sober today, and I learned how from others who are still sober, too.

On Finding the Necessary Number of Meetings (#2)

Whatever number of meetings you think you need to stay sober, add one.

This quotation is downright sneaky. It's also extremely effective. It refers to the Big Book, *Alcoholics Anonymous*, which discusses the "easier, softer way" that A.A. wisdom knows does not work for self-willed alcoholics. My sponsors would allow me to pick the number of necessary meetings I thought I should attend, but they recognized the tendency to "round down" the number; hence, the reason for the quotation.

The quote also reflects the awareness that sobriety, like liberty, has a high price: constant vigilance. We can't afford to be sloppy in picking our meetings and our sponsors, nor can we underestimate our lifetime commitment to sobriety. As my sponsors told me until I got sick of hearing it (and then I learned it and couldn't hear it enough): "One drink is too many, and a thousand isn't enough." Whatever it takes to avoid that one drink is what we must do.

On "Too Many Meetings"

Would you rather have him out four nights a week and sober or home seven nights a week and drunk?

This was said to a woman who complained she never saw her husband anymore. This was the same woman who only a few weeks before had said she didn't care if "I ever see that drunken bum again!" The question she was asked doesn't require an answer. Naturally, she preferred to see her husband sober.

There are A.A. members who have less than perfect marriages and use the A.A. meeting as an escape. One could say that this is going to too many meetings. There also are

A.A. members who don't have families and use A.A. as a substitute. I don't think that's so bad.

For the newly-sober, there's no such thing as "too many meetings."

MORE ABOUT MEETINGS

On Going to Beginners' Meetings

We're all beginners, we begin anew every morning. If you think you're too old or senior in the program for a beginners' meeting, you're in BIG trouble!

We must realize today is all we have. Yesterday is over and we may not see tommorow. So we are all beginners. We do start again each day.

The beginners' meeting format is a four-week rotation: one meeting each on Step One, Two, and Three, with a fourth meeting on the history of A.A. The meetings are simple, direct, and comfortable; they help ease the entry of the often shaky newcomer into the fellowship.

For these meetings to be most helpful for the newcomer, it is essential that some older members also be present to lend their experience and help.

On Open Meetings

Open meetings are great, but if they make up more than half of the meetings you go to, you're not working your program.

Open meetings, where outsiders are also welcome, are good meetings for new A.A. members to attend. They're a good way to meet other people, hear speakers, buy literature, and more. But because outsiders are present, open meetings tend not to be as instructive in emphasizing the meaning of the Twelve Steps and the traditions of A.A. as closed meetings so often are.

In closed meetings, newcomers who are skirting disaster are confronted with their actions and the potential consequences. Confidential experiences, which are most helpful to the newer member, are shared in closed meetings, but never in open meetings.

If one is still playing around with the idea of drinking, one is less likely to stand out at an open meeting which tends to have a larger number of people attending. Attitudes which lead to relapse may not be so obvious at an open meeting and thus not confronted until these attitudes have already done damage to one's sobriety.

On "Hiding Out" at Meetings

If you keep on going to meetings where nobody knows you, nobody will notice when you stop going — or when you die.

The caution is against going only to larger (usually open) meetings or "shopping around" for meetings until you get into the position where almost no one knows if you're attending meetings or not. This form of isolation is particularly dangerous to the newer member, but it can be a danger to any recovering alcoholic. The very nature of A.A. is a mutual caring and sharing group, whose members participate in each other's recovery because they share a common past.

The last part of the quotation refers to another piece of A.A. wisdom, namely that relapse is almost without exception preceded by dropping meetings, and then not going to any meetings. "Stinking thinking leads to stinking drinking" is another truism quoted by my sponsors over and over.

On Fears of Meeting Someone You Know at an A.A. Meeting

What the hell do you think they're there for? Ingrown toenails?

A common fear of newcomers is they will be identified as alcoholics by someone from their "real" life. A.A. respects the confidentiality of its members. A.A. is not a breeding ground for gossip, nor is it a news service. This is one of the attributes of the fellowship that can be believed only with experience.

A friend who is an attorney had finally decided to do something about his drinking and come to A.A. When he walked into his first home group meeting, there were two attorney acquaintances in the group who greeted him. "Hi there. We've been waiting for you!" Before he came to A.A. their anonymity, and his, had been respected.

A.A. life is the real life. Until the lessons and principles we learn in A.A. become part of our outside lives, we can't claim to be truly working the program. The Twelfth Step says it all: "practice these principles in all our affairs."

On Not Liking a Meeting

If you ever go to an A.A. meeting and you don't like it, look into the mirror to find out why

The premise here is that one should be able to get something valuable out of any meeting, and the only barrier to this is ourselves. We may be too prudish and refuse to go to a meeting because of bad language. We may object to meetings held in treatment centers. Or it could be we "don't want junkies at *our* meetings." Whatever reason we have for not liking a meeting, the bottom line is if we don't like a meeting it's because we've let something else get ahead of our sobriety. We may dislike a meeting because we're in a rotten mood that spoils our concentration on what the meeting is all about, namely, a group of folks who have gotten together to help one another stay away from the bottle for a while longer. We can't put our bad moods ahead of sobriety.

On Not Wanting to Go to a Meeting

The more certain you are that you don't need or want to go to a meeting, the more certain I am that you do.

Don't think denial of your alcoholism goes away with the first A.A. meeting. If you feel you don't have to go to a meeting, denial is often behind the feeling. Granted, not every alcoholic returned to drinking because he or she missed a single meeting, nor did every alcoholic permanently lose his or her sobriety because of a single drink. It's that very fact that makes skipping meetings or taking occasional single drinks so terribly dangerous. The natural thought to an alcoholic is, "I got away with missing a meeting, and I got away with having one drink. I'll bet I can handle two or three drinks." Where that type of thinking leads is obvious.

There are going to be times when you don't feel good or the boss has dumped a short deadline on you or your family is having a special occasion, and you need to skip a meeting. Always test the feeling to assure yourself there really is a need for missing a meeting, making sure it's not a sign of denial.

On a Home Group

One of your regular meetings should be your A.A. home, no matter where it meets.

In the part of the world where I got sober, we met in each other's homes, keeping our groups limited to ten to twelve people. I can't overstate the importance this had for me in my recovery, that is, to have had ten or a dozen people who really knew me and who really cared whether or not I showed up the next week. These were people I could trust with any information, no matter how personal, knowing it would never be repeated.

A.A. home groups need not be located in living rooms to be effective. For example, they can be in church basements, storefronts, or hospital cafeterias. What makes a home group effective is the attitude of its members. As my sponsors said to me, "A home group is a place where, if you break both legs, you crawl to get to. It is a bunch of people who, when you arrive from California after a week away, you go to before you go home." A friend once came to our home group on his way home from the hospital after the death of his infant daughter. He only said, "I can't talk, but I have to be here." He made it through the tragedy in a sober state, and he still is sober.

ABOUT SPEAKERS

On the Quality of a Speaker

*Any alcoholic who has been sober all day to-
day has something of value to tell you — all you
have to do is open your ears.*

This is another way of saying your troubles with A.A. are
often, if not always, revealed in the mirror. When a speaker
has taken 45 minutes to tell his or her story, and he or she
isn't yet up to the year 1937, it's only human to wonder if the
end of the talk will ever come. My sponsors reminded me it's
important for a speaker to share, and giving a talk is a part of
recovery that should not be denied.

They also reminded me that any drunk who is free of
John Barleycorn for this day does in fact have something to
tell me about how this was accomplished. That's the foundation of A A. — shared experience. The gift is there for the
taking, but you have to reach out to get it

On Speaking at a Meeting

*Something in what you have to say may make
all the difference in whether some poor drunk lives
or dies — and you never know.*

The "pass it on" theme occurs again and again in A.A.
The reverse of the quoted statement is also potentially true:
something we may want to say, but don't, might make the
difference.

In one of my early home groups there was a person
whom we thought was drinking again, but we didn't confront her. She was faced with the loss of sight in one eye;

21

since I am one-eyed, I was asked to talk to her. I did talk to her for a long time about how to live with one eye, but I didn't mention how to live without drinking. Shortly thereafter, she committed suicide. The thought of what might have been comes back to me from time to time, even now, some twelve years too late.

ABOUT THE PEOPLE IN ALCOHOLICS ANONYMOUS

On Kinds of A.A. Members

There are two kinds of people in A.A. — hard-noses and others. Hard-noses get well.

The implication is that "others" don't get well. For alcoholics, not getting well probably means a shortened life.

A "hard-nose," according to my sponsors, is someone who "sticks with the winners." Hard-noses go to meetings, stay in touch with sponsors, and take their programs very seriously. They place their sobriety ahead of everything else. They know there are no shortcuts, and no easier, softer ways to maintain sobriety.

The others, on the contrary, miss meetings, are "too busy" to make Twelfth Step calls, and are too embarrassed to speak in public. They don't take their programs seriously. This is a big mistake because they probably will never get well.

On Hard-Noses (#1)

Every hard-nose I've ever seen is still sober, and those who are dead died sober. Others just died.

It is realistic to think that any alcoholic who returns to drinking is not a hard-nose. Hard-noses don't relapse.

I have never seen this fail: an alcoholic who relapses after spending a year or so in the fellowship has, for several weeks or months, been skipping meetings or not keeping in touch with his or her sponsors.

My sponsors told me of an A.A. friend who was dying in an intensive care unit at a local hospital. Because he was being given oxygen to ease his breathing, his mouth was quite dry. A visitor asked him, "Would you like something to drink?" Even comatose and near death, the old alcoholic's mouth tightened shut! *That's* a hard-nose!

On Hard-Noses (#2)

> *You can always tell the hard-noses — they're the sober ones!*

When you walk into an A.A. meeting you've never been to, there are always some people there who stand out. There is a look about them; they stand a little bit straighter; they smile; they look good. These are the hard-noses, and they are the sober ones. They take time to greet the newcomer. They don't merely look at you, they *see* you. One feels less shaky around them.

I used to go to A.A. meetings in a nearby town, and I always saw another recovering alcoholic, Leo, at the literature table. Leo fit all the attributes of a hard-nose. He died a few months ago, at his desk, with the *Twenty-Four Hours a Day** book open in front of him. No one who knew him was surprised; it was so characteristic of this beloved hard-nose.

On Two-Steppers

> *Two-Steppers often wind up not only getting themselves drunk, but their pigeons, too — that's a double waste!*

A Two-Stepper is a person who jumps right into helping a newcomer, or pigeon, without working the Twelve Steps of A.A. Double relapses have followed these dangerous arrangements. There is a double message here: it's dangerous to

---

* *Twenty-Four Hours a Day* is published by Hazelden Educational Materials, Center City, MN. Order no. 1050.

anyone's sobriety not to work the Twelve Steps; and it's dangerous to anyone's sobriety to have a sponsor who is not stable in recovery and is not following a solid A.A. program.

On Thirteenth Stepping

It's rough enough getting sober without complicating it with sex; both of you are at risk of losing it — your sobriety, I mean!

A Thirteenth Stepper is a person who acts as a sponsor for a person of the opposite sex. This is considered a bad practice by many A.A. members because the wisdom of A.A. is that the new member should not make any unnecessary changes in his or her life for the first year. Nothing must be allowed to supplant sobriety as the number one priority, and having a love affair with another recovering alcoholic has a way of becoming all-important.

ABOUT THE TWELVE STEPS OF ALCOHOLICS ANONYMOUS

On Working the Steps

Hard-noses speak of "working" the Steps.

If one thinks following the Twelve Steps is anything but hard work, one's chances for recovery are not good. To take each Step, to think about it over and over again, to extract the last bit of learning out of it, to stay with one Step until you are sure you understand it well — this is work. This is how hard-noses come to understand the fellowship of A.A. This is how they learn to live sober.

On the Need for Working the Steps

If you take the booze away from a drunken S.O.B., what's left is an S.O.B. Unless something is done about it, you'll have a drunken S.O.B. again, you can count on it — that's what the Steps are all about, changing the S.O.B.

The Twelve Steps confront one's self-righteous pride. We see language in the Twelve Steps — words such as "wrongs," "defects of character," "shortcomings," and "harmed" — aimed at producing humility and at pricking our sense of our own importance. We are advised to do things that at first may embarrass us, such as making direct amends, and admitting to another person exactly what kind of S.O.B.s we were during our drinking days. The miracle is that we are promised there will be positive changes happening to us as we continue working the Steps.

27

On Working the Steps in Order

*The Steps are in that order for the best of all
possible reasons — they work that way!*

There is a divine logic in the order of the Twelve Steps. As
we work each Step, we look deeper and deeper into ourselves. It's not possible to work Steps One through Twelve
without experiencing a profound, positive change. This is
why the hard-noses insist on "working," not "doing" the
Steps.

To try to work the Steps out of order is to fail. One cannot
make a list of those one has harmed, for example, if one has
not first taken a moral inventory. How can we do anything in
a "searching and fearless" way until we have abandoned fear
by turning our will and our lives over to the care of a Higher
Power? The process can't be hurried; there aren't any shortcuts. Step Two follows Step One, and Step Three follows Step
Two, in a natural and important progression.

On Understanding Step Two

*A good way to understand Step Two is to read
it like this: "Came, came to, came to believe."*

Recovery is complicated when the alcohol fumes have
barely left the brain. Hence, my sponsors' use of the first
three words of Step Two: "Came to believe." Another way
they made things clear was to say, "Take the body to a meeting. Eventually the brain will come along, too."

In addressing belief in a Higher Power, Step Two is difficult for many alcoholics to grasp. Some have lost their faith,
some never had any, and some cannot accept that a Higher
Power would take direct, personal interest in their recovery.

The language of the Step does not include the word
"God." Each alcoholic can have many Higher Powers. A recovering alcoholic might understand and use the A.A. group
as a Higher Power.

28

The point is, no matter how we understand a Higher Power, it takes time for some of us to gain enough spiritual understanding to accept that God, by whatever name we choose to use, does intervene for us individually and personally.

On Summarizing the First Three Steps

A simplified summary of the first three Steps is:
I can't, He can, I'm going to let Him.

This quote puts the first three Steps in a simple perspective that even a new A.A. recruit can understand. The first three Steps have to do with a personal statement of powerlessness, a belief that a Higher Power can and will intervene in our behalf, and a decision to turn our wills and our lives over to this Higher Power. They are often called entry Steps or beginning Steps (beginners' meetings usually concentrate on them). Newcomers often have difficulty adjusting to the ego-shattering concepts contained in them. Some of us old-timers do, too!

Powerlessness and unmanageability mean that we need to admit we can't hold our liquor, as well as confess our entire lives are like a runaway steamroller.

Many of us saw ourselves as invincible, invulnerable, and omniscient while under the influence of alcohol. Now we are asked to see that we are something a whole lot less than heroic.

Admitting we need to be restored to sanity is a bitter pill to swallow. The more sober we get, however, the less a problem this is for us to accept.

In order to get sober, we must turn ourselves over to a Power greater than ourselves. A.A.'s slogan is: "Get out of the driver's seat."

ABOUT BEING SICK, AND ABOUT RECOVERY

On the Disease Concept of Alcoholism

*I don't know whether it's a moral weakness or
a disease. All I know is that for me it's a FACT!*

A.A. accepts the disease concept; most medical authorities accept it, too. But some alcoholics, because of their behavior and actions during their drinking days, see their condition as having moral overtones.

The quote was not made by a sponsor, but by a close A.A. friend. We were at an A.A. meeting and the question of moral failing versus disease was being discussed. The debate was getting more and more heated until my friend made his statement. It ended the controversy. We all realized that what we do about our drinking is of paramount importance.

My sponsors told me not to ask "Why?" I learned that the cause of my alcoholism isn't as important as its existence. I still don't know for sure why I became an alcoholic, but it doesn't matter. I'm sober, thanks to God and the fellowship, and that does matter.

On Anonymity

*I don't care who knows I'm an alcoholic, so
long as I don't ever forget it!*

A.A.'s tradition of anonymity is often misunderstood, and this quote is an attempt to set the record straight. What my sponsors understood is that, at the level of the media, anonymity is a cornerstone of the fellowship of A.A. But for some alcoholics, anonymity can be used as a hiding place — a way to deny their alcoholism.

My sponsors taught me to let every person I meet know quickly and very clearly that I don't drink. "The idea is it'll make it that much more difficult for you to belly up to the bar again," they said. And they were right once again.

On Controlled Drinking

For an alcoholic? Don't make me laugh!

Every few years, someone comes up with a magic system by which alcoholics can be taught to drink again. Statistics are cited that "prove" a certain percentage of alcoholics can be taught to drink "responsibly" again. A.A. absolutely denies this, using the premise that if a person really can be taught to drink responsibly, he or she wasn't an alcoholic in the first place. This makes good sense to recovering alcoholics, but some people don't think it's a very strong argument.

Every one of the studies on controlled drinking I've examined has two failings. First, the samples are very small, meaning the sample of alcoholics who return to responsible drinking is very small. Second, the studies do not keep track of the alcoholics in the sample for very long. The best single study I have seen tracked, for a period of five years, consisted of 100 alcoholics who had returned to drinking. At the end of five years, every alcoholic in the sample had either died, was institutionalized, or had attained sobriety. This is conclusive for me. Abstinence is the best way to prevent alcoholism from progressing to its natural termination — which could be your termination.

On Recovery

You didn't get that sick overnight, and it's going to take awhile to get well. Relax and work today's program today.

Once the alcohol fumes are out of our heads, we see life can be beautiful, and we may find we want it all *now*. We don't yet have the long-term sobriety to see that we need a careful foundation of recovery to withstand the bad experiences that happen in life. If we build a hasty, sloppy foundation, that's the sort of recovery program we'll have. If we try to jump into Twelfth Step work too soon, we're going to make a mess of it. But if we keep on working today's program today, we'll establish a good, strong recovery. Then we'll be able to help ourselves. Then we'll be able to help others. The things we should do today may not always seem important to recovery, but each Step in our recovery program is important.

On Being Recovered

The only difference between a recovered and a recovering alcoholic is that the recovering alcoholic is still breathing.

For as long as we live, recovery is a process which can be stopped anytime by picking up a drink; hence, the hard-nosed insistence on the word "recovering." It may seem picky, but to the hard-noses in A.A., the bottom line is that, for as long as we live, recovery is not certain. I had a friend who recovered after he died. He's still helping me with my recovery, because I remember him each time I pass his grave. Some alcoholics call themselves "recovered" and it doesn't seem to hurt them any; but I'm not going to take any chances with my recovery. I am a "recovering" alcoholic, and I hope it's a long time before I'm "recovered."

ABOUT SOBRIETY

On the Proper Place for Sobriety

If your sobriety isn't your absolute top priority, the most important thing in your life, you're going to get drunk again.

This may seem too harsh, but it's actually kindness in disguise. The natural and immediate reaction is to reject the idea that your sobriety must outweigh everything else in your life. The fact of the matter is that wives, husbands, jobs, faith, family, health, and wealth all dissolve in alcohol. At whatever stage in recovery, an alcoholic owes it all to sobriety.

There are dangers of coming to A.A. for any reason other than a desire to stop drinking. That's why A.A. counsels against radical changes in one's life for at least the first year of recovery.

A nonalcoholic whom I highly respect has complained to me that much of A.A.'s teaching has a sort of "or else" flavor about it, and he finds this to be a negative thing. My answer is that it isn't negative and it isn't intended to frighten. It's realistic.

On Counting One's Sobriety

Hard-noses count their sobriety by one of only two acceptable ways, either by the first meeting after the last drink, or by the solitary word "today." The harder the nose the more likely it is by "today" that they count.

A.A. members are not really superstitious, but it sometimes seems that way. Many will not claim anything more than "a few 24 hours" for their sobriety. No one who is trying to be honest claims a period of sobriety which preceded the last drinking lapse. Others often do, but they don't fool anyone but themselves. It's as though to claim a fixed period of time for sobriety is to brag about something we have only as a gift. When I asked my sponsors how long they had been sober, they often responded, "All day."

"Today" makes very good sense as a yardstick to measure sobriety. Today's sobriety is what will keep me clean, not yesterday's, and not tomorrow's.

On Longevity in A.A.

At any A.A. meeting, the person with the greatest longevity in the program is the person who got up first that morning.

This quote is about living in the "now" of things. A twenty-year A.A. member is ranked no higher or lower than a first-meeting member. For each of them, the only sobriety they can count on and bet their lives on is the sobriety they enjoy today.

I've attended meetings where it was rather important to some of the members to claim "numbers" on each other. I found it petty and not in harmony with the traditions of A.A. After all, what difference does it make? What's important is that either you're sober or you're not.

Those who claim large numbers of years in the program are often playing games with themselves. Someone who claims to have been "around" the program for a certain number of years probably hasn't been *in* the program that long. One is either in the program or one is not. One is never "around" the program.

On the Basic Truth about Sobriety

Things do *get better!*

When we come to A.A., things seem as bad as can be. We are at the bottom of a deep hole, and there appears no way out. Our self-image and our sense of well-being are pretty well shot. Our hands are shaky enough to raise whitecaps on coffee, and the look in our eyes is better left to the imagination.

If we continue to attend A.A. meetings and try to work the Twelve Steps, we'll gradually feel and look better. We'll learn to laugh, particularly at ourselves. We'll sleep like babies at night, not like the dead. Things in our lives will begin to get better, too. Bosses will tend to make fewer remarks about unemployment; people will seem to enjoy our company, and we'll find ourselves with energy we may not have felt for years. In short, we'll look into the mirror and no longer feel an overwhelming desire to puke. Things aren't always good, but all in all, things do get better.

On the Present

> Now *is all we have. The past is just that and the future is out of reach. If we make a deal with ourselves to stay sober* now, *and keep it, we're home free.*

A.A. teachings again and again emphasize the need to live in the present, to avoid projecting on the future, or dwelling on the past. We can do nothing about our program, about our sobriety, about our recovery, except *now*. Whatever we did or didn't do yesterday is done. It either helped or hindered our recovery, but it's beyond our capacity to change in any way.

We can either fear or look forward to tomorrow. We can prepare for it or not. But we can't do the slightest thing about tomorrow's recovery. We can't take a drink tomorrow, or refrain from taking one. As my sponsors said, if we can get a handle on staying sober today, we're home free.

ABOUT THE OLD AND THE NEW YOU IN ALCOHOLICS ANONYMOUS

On Changing Your Ways

> *If you keep on doing what you used to do,*
> *you'll keep on getting what you used to get.*

This quote came to me from a recovering priest, not from my sponsors, but it's too good to leave out. What you used to get was drunk, and this quote is strong advice to change the spots on your alcoholic leopard, or you'll get drunk again. Cheating on your expense account, on your wife or husband, or on your income taxes is all the same; if that's what you were doing you'd better do something about it, or those old ways will trip you up again.

The moral inventory we are asked to make in Step Four does not contain the words "searching and fearless" for nothing. We have to search deeply, or we simply won't do a thorough job; a sloppy job is almost always worse than a job not done at all. "Fearless" means we must not allow fear to keep us from being searching and thorough, because the alternative to sobriety does not bear thinking about.

On Being Tempted

> *What the hell were you doing there in the first*
> *place?*

Very early in my recovery, as I walked to the train, I passed a favorite liquor store that was advertising my favorite brand. With some effort and self-pity and a great deal of self-righteousness, I managed not to go in. When I got to the train, my sponsor was there, and I told him what had happened. The statement I've quoted was his response. I was crushed. I thought he'd at least pat me on the back. But then I gave some serious thought to what he was saying to me, and I realized I had made things harder for myself. I didn't need to go near a liquor store. He challenged me to find a way to walk from my office to the train without passing a liquor store or a tavern. That isn't easy in a big city like Chicago, but it can be done, and he made me find out how.

We often create difficult situations for ourselves. We often get in the way of our sobriety. My sponsor was showing me I really hadn't put my sobriety first. He recognized what I had yet to learn: an alcoholic never needs to be looking in a liquor store window. Potentially dangerous situations are easily handled when we don't let them take place.

On Being Caught Short Away from Home

You can always pee in a gas station or a McDonald's — you never need to be in a tavern.

Using the rest room of a tavern under most circumstances seems harmless. But if we never go into a tavern, we'll never buy a drink in a tavern.

When I had been sober for nearly a year, my wife had to leave town, and there was some booze in the house. I asked her to give it away or throw it away, so I couldn't possibly get into trouble with it. I had no craving, no desire, but I recognized a possible problem. It was easier to solve the problem this way than to risk everything on my frail strength.

On Buying Cigarettes

If you have to smoke, at least buy your cigarettes in a drugstore, not in a liquor store, no matter how much cheaper they are.

If you are both a smoker and a recovering alcoholic, the wisdom of A.A. is, "Take care of one addiction at a time." My sponsors thought the effort of achieving stable sobriety was so important that they didn't recommend I stop smoking at the same time. "Wait awhile," they said, "get your drinking out of the way first. Then, when you're sober, you can afford to think about your smoking." Sobriety must not share the top spot on your priorities list with anything, or else you may not maintain it. Most successful ex-smokers I know (and that includes myself) used the Twelve Step program for overcoming that addiction, too. But all of them waited until they were sober to quit smoking.

On Hanging Out with the Old Gang

You need new playgrounds and new play-mates.

My first sponsors recommended I tell all of my friends I had stopped drinking. One friend dropped me after I told him, and I think it was because I threatened him by my sobriety. If I had a drinking problem, he may have thought he did, too, and he couldn't handle that. All of my true friends were unanimously glad I had quit. They had been praying for me, or worried they'd have to go to my funeral. My news to them was nothing but heaven-sent. My sponsors didn't tell me to stay away from taverns and wild parties; they told me to find new playgrounds and new playmates. Alcoholics have friends who are still in alcoholic mind-sets. We need to avoid this because it's familiar and comfortable to us, and dangerous to our newfound sobriety. "Feel depressed? Get drunk and it'll all go away!" That's an example of the way we thought and of the way some of our old playmates still think. We simply cannot afford that sort of thinking.

On Expecting Praise for Being in A.A.

You shouldn't expect a medal for finally doing what you were supposed to do in the first place.

Many of us, including myself, feel at first that the world should applaud us for joining A.A. What we're actually doing is saving our own skins. Self-preservation is a survival skill of normal people. When we finally get around to a little self-preservation instead of self-destruction, we have no right to expect admiration from society.

We join A.A. not for the approval of others, but for our own survival. We stay in A.A. to continue breathing, not to get public acclaim. If we are in A.A. for public notice, we're high risks to get drunk again.

ABOUT HIGHER POWERS
AND PRAYER

On Belief in a Higher Power

*Don't sweat it. Keep on bringing your body to
a meeting and eventually your brain will come
along, too.*

I've already used the above quote in talking about understanding Step Two. The quote bears repeating because our
sobriety will be shallow and fragile without understanding
and believing in a Higher Power. Some alcoholics are satisfied
with a concept of electricity or nuclear energy or a steam
radiator as Higher Powers. They reason that these are incomprehensible to them and stronger than they are. Electricity,
nuclear energy, and steam radiators, however, didn't help me
get sober, and I will not recognize as a Higher Power anything
that didn't help me.

My sponsors are part of my Higher Power, God, as I
choose to understand Him. My home group helped me get
sober, and it's a Higher Power to me; I recognize my home
group's actions as God's actions. A.A. helped me get sober,
and it's also a Higher Power to me. I firmly believe God
inspired Bill W. and Dr. Bob. It's not important that you accept or reject the notion of God as your Higher Power, but it
is supremely important to understand that when two or more
alcoholics are gathered together, a group is a Higher Power
for everybody in it; the group knows more about living sober
than any single member.

On Religion and A.A.

It's perfectly all right to go to church, and it may even help your recovery, but it isn't necessary.

A.A. is a spiritual program of recovery, but it is not associated with any religious denomination. If A.A. were a Christian organization, where would Jewish, Buddhist, Moslem, and atheistic alcoholics go? A.A.'s cofounders kept religion out of the fellowship, thereby assuring its success.

The distinction between spirituality and religion, however, bothers many people. A.A. members recognize that judging others is something they are not qualified to do. Keeping an alcoholic away from the fellowship because of a religious belief amounts to judging that alcoholic. We can't do that, and that's why A.A. has no connection (and seeks none) with any religious denomination.

I have experienced Christian love in A.A. meetings; I've also been around some of the least religious people I know at those same meetings.

The criticism that A.A. is nonreligious should be answered as follows: there are good reasons for the separation of church and state, and there are equally good reasons for the separation of church and A.A.

On the Grace of God

Whenever you see a drunk, remember that it is, but for the grace of God, yourself you see.

We may have a tendency to dwell on our accomplishments. This is silly, particularly with respect to recovery from alcoholism. For some incomprehensible reason, in some inexplicable way, God (by whatever way we understand God) gave us recovery. Therefore, the only difference between us and the drunks we see around us is not some superiority of ours, but the grace of God.

Some theologians have trouble with the concept of the grace of God; arguments abound. Alcoholics in recovery have

44

no trouble at all with the concept. As we come into contact with those yet drunk, we must keep the thought in our minds that we are no better. But for some reason (which has nothing to do with our merits) we are more blessed than them. If our main response to that isn't gratitude, we're headed for another drink.

On the Serenity Prayer

If you're in a real pinch, try the short form of the Serenity Prayer: "Screw it." You'll be surprised how effective it can be.

The beloved Serenity Prayer, as used by A.A., is said as follows: "God grant me the serenity to accept the things I cannot change; the courage to change the things I can; and wisdom to know the difference." The short form of the Serenity Prayer as quoted is not irreverent. It is a prayer. It is a way of saying, "I can't stop to be formal right now. I'm in a bad place and I need to get rid of these bad feelings. Help me understand that 'This, too, will pass,' and stay with me until it does."

From time to time, things happen with no warning. Until we develop our A.A. muscles, we need something to help us through the unpredictable crises; the short form is an excellent way. It is short and sweet, it shows a certain amount of wry humor, and, most important of all, it works!

On Manners

As a child, you learned to say "please" and "thank-you." Let your first prayer of the day be a "please" for sobriety, and your last prayer of the night be a "thank-you" for a sober day.

My sponsors believe we have a right to ask for help in staying sober. This doesn't mean we're entitled to ask God to keep us sober; we can ask for help, but the job is ours. There is a proverb from my home country — "Pray for potatoes, but grab a hoe" — that says the same thing. An even older saying

is: "Without God, we cannot; without us, God will not."
We ask for God's help, not his performance; that's our
department.

We must also have gratitude. We beg for help, and it is
forthcoming. If we fail to acknowledge the gift, it may be
withdrawn, and by now we can be certain where that leads.

So, then, every morning we should pray: "Please help me
to stay sober today." And every night: "Thank-you for a sober
day."

On the Answering of Prayers

*If you pray right, your prayers are answered.
Of course, if you pray wrong, they're answered,
too.*

Praying right, to my sponsors, is praying daily for help
with sobriety, coupled with gratitude for the help received.
As they pointed out, these prayers have a way of being
answered positively each time. By following the advice of my
sponsors, I have had my prayers answered affirmatively for
almost 5,000 consecutive days.

On the other hand, prayers such as, "I'll do anything you
want if you'll only get me out of this mess," are general-
ly considered by my sponsors to be prayers that are badly
directed.

There's a story of a little girl whose birthday was ap-
proaching; her father heard her praying for a puppy. She
didn't get a puppy on her birthday, and her father teased her
about her prayer being unanswered. Her reply was, "God *did*
answer my prayer. He said, 'No.' " If we expect a deity or any
other source to get us sober and keep us that way, we're
doomed to disappointment. These prayers are answered, but
negatively. For the alcoholic, this means staying in the alcoholic quagmire and very possibly dying in it.

ABOUT ANTABUSE AND TREATMENT

On the Advisability of Taking Antabuse

Sure it's a crutch, but a crutch is very useful if you have a broken leg. Eventually, broken legs heal.

Antabuse is a drug that makes it nearly impossible to drink alcohol. The metabolism of alcohol into carbon dioxide and water is interrupted by Antabuse at the acetaldehyde stage; acetaldehyde is a toxic substance which, given high enough levels, produces a range of unpleasant symptoms. Antabuse has been prescribed most often for alcoholics who have been unsuccessful in stopping drinking.

Opinion on using Antabuse varies widely. Some alcoholics think it's not appropriate to use; they rely instead on the A.A. program. Others point out that, at some time, the alcoholic must get off the drug. Others think it's great. Treatment professionals also disagree. My sponsors' point is that there are times, particularly when an alcoholic has a history of relapses, when Antabuse is appropriate. An alcoholic may not be able to abstain long enough to understand A.A.'s message, so we are grateful that Antabuse is available. It's a temporary measure, to be sure, and the Antabuse user needs to understand that Antabuse is not a lifelong prescription nor a substitute for A.A. membership.

There are legends about Antabuse. Some old-timers will claim to have used alcohol and Antabuse at the same time; they say they drink and get sick and drink and get sick,

47

and at some point they drink and don't get sick. Others claim the bad effects of Antabuse pass after awhile.

If Antabuse is in your system, you can't pretend it isn't and drink. There will be a reaction and it is definitely an unpleasant one. Those who brag about drinking while on Antabuse are those who were dragged into A.A. kicking and screaming, if they ever got the message.

On Quitting or Refusing Antabuse Therapy

Thirsty, huh?

The refusal to use Antabuse if recommended by a doctor, or quitting it against medical advice, are identified by my sponsors as signs of denial. My sponsors went to the heart of the matter with the two words I've quoted. The person to whom this was said had just gone through a half hour of persuasive explanation as to why he shouldn't take Antabuse. In A.A., this is called "intellectualization," or "rationalization," and it's frowned upon. I wish I could tell you that the pigeon never drank again, but the truth is I don't know what happened to him.

On the Efficiency of Therapy

If it works, don't fool around with it; if it doesn't, quit.

Many A.A. members have a mixed bag of feelings about doctors and therapists. This is probably because many doctors and therapists, if not most of them, simply do not understand alcoholism. Horror stories abound about psychiatrists who allow drunks to drink while under their care, about social workers who are pleased that so-and-so has cut down to only one fifth per day, or about doctors who fall for hard luck stories or outright lies and prescribe Valium.

My sponsors recognize the truth of A.A.'s slogan, "If it works, don't fix it," and made the statement I've quoted to

a pigeon who was being counseled by well-meaning members of our A.A. group. Some wanted him to continue therapy; others wanted him to quit.

A.A. practices a sort of benevolent pragmatism; this is why members practice their own programs, while admitting their programs might not work for others. There's the attitude, "Whether therapy would or would not work for me is immaterial; it just doesn't matter. What matters is if it works for you."

ABOUT COCKTAIL PARTIES

On Going to a Cocktail Party

If you can skip it, do.

There have been a number of clever articles written about cocktail party conversation; for example, how to confess to a multiple axe murder and receive the response, "That's nice."

Like taverns, cocktail parties present a potential source of danger to an alcoholic. Because the purpose of a cocktail party is for drinking, such "entertainment" is not essential to our health and well-being. If they can be avoided, they should be.

For an alcoholic, the next best thing to not going to a cocktail party is to arrive as late as you can and leave as soon as possible. By a cocktail party, my sponsors meant one of those stand-up things that last from 4:00 to 6:00 P.M., or from 5:00 to 7:00 P.M., which never end on time. They're usually held in a room with insufficient air circulation and oversufficient population, with too much smoke and not enough chairs, and their purpose is drinking, no matter how disguised (benefit, reception, etc.).

There's another thing about cocktail parties that's very apparent to a nondrinker: they're boring! For a while, I had to make duty appearances at a periodic party which many of the same people attended each time. I could set my watch by the telling of a particular joke, or by the departure of a particular foursome into the kitchen (where the bar was). There was a sense of *déjà vu* in hearing the same conversations

51

from the same mouths; if I hadn't been so busy being bored, I might have been embarrassed.

For any alcoholic at any time, if what you plan to do threatens your sobriety in any way, don't do it!

My sponsors have nothing against a party, and neither do I. A gathering of congenial people, with or without alcohol, is a different affair than the uncivilized thing called a "cocktail party." If you want to see a really good party, drop in on an A.A. party. We have picnics, camp-ins, and formal dinner-dances. They're lots of fun; there's plenty of laughter, and no hangovers.

On Behavior at a Cocktail Party

Get a glass of something safe in your hand and nurse it; nobody will really give a damn what's in your glass, as long as you have one.

What you're holding is completely irrelevant. But when your hands are empty, it sets up a situation that can be dangerous. Empty hands are a host's or hostess's reproach; they seem to bring out the pusher in otherwise nice folks.

For example, your hostess may think she is being clever and bring you a glass of what she thought you were drinking, and she may have thought wrong. Or a host might start an argument about what you want to drink, and catch you at a weak moment. Or you may have a weak moment all by yourself.

Here's a tip: Don't hold an empty glass like it's empty. Hold it carefully, as though you were afraid it might spill.

On Safe Beverages at a Cocktail Party

A hot drink such as coffee is the safest. Never drink anything cold at a cocktail party that you don't watch poured.

Waiters do make mistakes from time to time. But it's real hard to make a mistake with a cup of coffee. Seven-Up looks like gin and tonic, especially with a lime twist, and the difference between Coke and rum and Coke is not discernible to the naked eye. To insist on watching the drink poured is not paranoia, but appropriate caution for an alcoholic.

I remember when I was in an Air Force officer's club with a crew of nonalcoholics. We ordered our first drinks at the bar, then took them to a table. I was drinking Coke. It happened to be a two-for-one night, and the second round was brought by a waiter. My Coke looked like Coke, but it had a cherry in it. My sponsors' remark came to mind, and I didn't drink it.

One exception to this rule is in the coach section of an airplane. If the flight attendant doesn't ask for money for your drink, it's nonalcoholic!

On Being Asked, "What'll Ya Have?"

Tell them coffee, or a Coke.

The newly sober alcoholic is often vulnerable, and the aggressive host's or hostess's inquiry can be intimidating. What my sponsors taught me is that I don't ever have to drink. For me to accept a drink so as not to offend a host or hostess is extremely hazardous to my health. It is far more polite to be firm and assertive, and refuse an alcoholic beverage. It has become more and more the rule to offer attractive alternatives to alcoholic beverages, and so it is less of an effort to choose something safe.

My sponsors told me the decision to abstain is mine; it is not and should not be, even for a little while, the decision of another person. My wife understands this; she will not answer for me, although she doesn't want me to drink. It's my place to refuse a drink, not hers.

On Being Pressed, "What Do You Want in It?"

Tell them, "A little cream," or, "Some ice," depending on what you asked for.

The lesson here is to be assertive, and not to compromise.

If your host or hostess doesn't hear you the first time, or refuses to hear you, make sure that the message gets across. After all, it's your neck. When I fly, I am often asked, "Do you want a drink?" I sometimes answer, "Yes, I would. But I'm an alcoholic, so I choose not to." To put it mildly, this gets the attendant's attention. Most of the time, I get great service from then on, and all of the coffee I can handle! I guess they have enough experience with people who shouldn't drink but do, and they're appreciative of those of us who abstain.

The host or hostess who knows you're a recovering person will not press you. Some hosts and hostesses who are aware of what I am and what I'm doing about it, will ask me if I want a drink in order to give me the opportunity to refuse. I consider this exquisite manners, because they are joining my efforts by allowing me to make the necessary choices for my sobriety.

ABOUT SLIPS

On Slips

The word "slip" implies an accident. There-
fore, there are no slips in A.A. We set ourselves up
to go back to drinking and then we pretend it's all
a mistake. Baloney and horseradish!

Incidentally, the words my sponsors used were not "baloney" and "horseradish."

The hard-nose recognizes that there is a part of us (no
matter how long since our last drink) that wants to go back to
drinking. If we deny this, we're getting close to our next
drink.

To stay sober, we should go to meetings regularly, practice
the A.A. principles in all our affairs, and keep in touch with
our sponsors.

On Starting a Slip

The first step in going back to drinking is to
question the very things which helped us to get
sober.

This questioning usually precedes by some months an
actual return to drinking. My sponsors used to say, "Everybody who is in A.A. for the first time got here by their own
individual route, their own story. Everyone in A.A. for the
second time or more has come here by the same story."

A slip starts with questioning the A.A. program of recovery. "I don't need to take the Fourth (or Sixth, or whatever)
Step." "I am an adult. I don't need a keeper (sponsor)." "I
don't want to go on Twelfth Step calls." And so on.

What happens next is completely predictable. The alcoholic skips some meetings and the sky doesn't fall in, so he or she skips more meetings, and then stops going to A.A. completely. Somewhere along this slide into oblivion a drink is taken and nothing happens, so the next time two drinks are taken, then four. And so on.

Those who are lucky get another chance. The others don't.

On the Consequences of a Slip

Alcoholics who relapse hold their lives in their own shaky hands.

The disease of alcoholism is so powerful that almost anything can happen. I know an alcoholic who allowed himself one drink following a well-earned job promotion. When he came to, he discovered he had spent a week in a chair in his basement, awaking only long enough to get blasted again. What scared him most was that he had never gotten drunk like that before!

A.A. polls its members every three years or so, and has some remarkable and consistent statistics. One of these statistics is called 4:2:1, which means that of every four people who come to A.A., two never drink again; and of the two who do drink again, one eventually gets sober in A.A. I was fortunate and haven't had a drink since my first meeting — as we say, "by the grace of God and the fellowship of A.A."

There's a darker side to this statistic in the fact that of the two who return to drinking, one doesn't make it. In other words, the alcoholic who relapses faces a 50-50 chance of never coming back.

On Admitting a Slip

If you don't take your "slip" to your home group, you're setting yourself up for another one.

Chapter Five of the Big Book, *Alcoholics Anonymous,* contains two words that have given a lot of us trouble at one time or another. Those two words are: "rigorous honesty." It means we shouldn't lie about our drinking and we shouldn't hold back about our drinking, most particularly with our home groups. To do so is to be dishonest and to be in real present danger of yet another relapse.

There is something one might call a "therapeutic relapse." My sponsors are of the opinion that a relapse can be made into a therapeutic one by sharing it with the home group, so the person who relapses can learn from the wisdom and the experience of the other members of the group. I have seen this in the "Son-of-a-gun, you were right!" sort of experience some alcoholics have.

Alcoholics may receive all the necessary instructions from their sponsors, but these instructions may not have any inner reality to them. So they relapse, and then they may finally see the light. This is encouraging, and their chances for recovery are pretty good. Relapse, however, is very risky. Remember, it's a 50-50 chance you won't come back, and those odds aren't very good. If a relapse can possibly be avoided, do what has to be done to avoid it.

ABOUT TWELFTH STEPPING AND SPONSORSHIP

On Why to Go on Twelfth Step Calls

It helps to keep you sober.

A.A. is full of paradoxes. We have no leaders, yet we're well led. We have no budget, yet we get along. We have a selfish program, yet the best way to keep the program is to give it away.

This is what Twelfth Step calls are all about: giving the program away to someone else, passing it along. Although the program was given to us, it's not our private property, and it's something we should pass along. When we do this, we find that we know the program more strongly than ever.

Outsiders and A.A. newcomers sometimes miss the boat and look at a Twelfth Step call as either a rescue mission, a sales pitch, or a marketing endeavor. Someone once asked one of my sponsors, "You must have been on a thousand Twelfth Step calls. How many were successful?" Without batting an eye, my sponsor said, "All of them. I came away sober from each one." Of course, we hope that the person we visit finds recovery in the A.A. program, but the real motive is the strengthening of our own programs. If this weren't our motive, we'd start getting picky — you know, only going on calls that seemed promising, so we could boast of an impressive string of accomplishments. That's not what Twelfth Step calls are about, and that's not what the entire A.A. program is about, either.

On Not Wanting to Go on a Twelfth Step Call

Someone was there for you; where would you be if they hadn't been?

We know where we'd be — probably dead. But A.A. cautions us against thinking of a Twelfth Step call as a debt that must be paid. First, if it were a debt, we could pay it off by making one or two calls, which denies the true purpose of such a call. Second, we should not go from a sense of obligation; rather, we should go and talk about ourselves and answer a few questions. We might do a little persuasion, but we aren't trained counselors — we're drunks who have learned (at least for a while) to live without drinking.

And yet, we'd have been in a hell of a mess, to put it mildly, if there hadn't been someone there for us. We really can't afford, if we have a healthy conscience, to fail to answer the call whenever we can. Yes, it's okay to refuse to go on a call — you won't be kicked out of A.A. But for your sobriety's sake, your excuse had better be real strong. My sponsor told me he almost refused to go on a Twelfth Step call because he was super-tired. He went anyway, and found that the pigeon was his sponsor's only son!

On Calling One's Sponsor

If you call me at three A.M. when you're drunk and tell me you can't sleep, I'll tell you I can and hang up on you.

The purpose of a sponsor is to be a combination of a teacher, guide, cop, friend, and role model. The purpose of a sponsor is not to be an alcoholism counselor. My sponsor's remark illustrates this point. I do know some alcoholics who called their sponsors when they had been drinking, and the sponsors hung up on them. The time to use a sponsor wisely is when the urge to drink has just appeared, not when it has succeeded. Implicit in the remark I've quoted is the teaching that a sponsor is there to talk with regularly and to go to meetings with, but not to use as a crisis line.

On What to Do about a Drunken Pigeon

> *If it's too cool, you might throw a blanket over him.*

I was present when the wife of a man, who was having some difficulty in getting the A.A. message, called to report that her husband had gotten into the whiskey sours and was passed out on the dining room floor. My sponsor made the remark I've quoted, and then he held the receiver away from his ear. Loud noises came from it. The alcoholic was throwing up. When the noises subsided, my sponsor said to the alcoholic's wife, "If you help him upstairs, in the morning he'll be able to deny the whole thing took place. Leave him on the floor — he won't be able to deny that. If you're really concerned about him, you might put a pillow under his head, but if he doesn't have to face the consequences of his drinking behavior, he'll never get sober." He added that the pigeon should talk to him in the morning. As of this writing, that particular pigeon has been sober for more than twelve years.

Alcoholics are so needy and dependent it's difficult to avoid rescuing them from the consequences of their drinking. But rescuing them only enables them to drink some more.

ABOUT GOOD DAYS AND BAD ONES

On Good Days and Bad Days

> *Any alcoholic who can put his or her head on the pillow at night sober has had a good day, no matter what else has gone wrong.*

It seemed to me that I had had some pretty bad days since I joined A.A., but this quote denied it. I began to see that for an alcoholic, a sober day is the best there is; anything added to the sober day is icing on the cake. So, if everything takes on a bad color, and all the icing is stripped off my cake, I can still have a good day, because I'm sober.

On Best Days and Worst Days

> *Your worst day sober is better than you best day drunk.*

"Sure, sure," I'd think, "that's easy for *you* to say." But to be absolutely logical about it (and try to do that when you're drunk!), if it takes sobriety to have a good day, then the truth of this quotation is obvious. No matter what experiences we might have had, our drunk days were self-destructive days, and never good ones.

On Days that Really Go Bad

> *There's nothing so bad for an alcoholic that a drink won't make worse.*

"Think of the worst possible thing that could happen to you," my sponsors said. "Imagine that this hideous thing has just happened to you, and you go to a bar to drown your sorrows. Will drinking do anything about your situation? Will it make it any better? Of course not!"

I used to blame job pressures for my drinking. But all drinking did for me was to make me miss deadlines and appointments. Drinking increased the pressures I felt. When I didn't blame the job, I blamed my domestic situation. If you think for a moment that drinking helps things at home, you're crazy.

ABOUT LAST WORDS

On Miracles

*Don't tell me there aren't any more miracles;
just look around the room!*

The odds against an alcoholic are horrendous. By a wide
margin, most alcoholics who don't practice recovery will die
of alcoholism or its effects. Medical treatment alone won't
solve the problem, neither will counseling nor any of the
other helping professions. The helpless alcoholic, drowning
in despair, can be thought of as a lost cause. Almost certainly,
this person is doomed. And yet, the message drunks carry to
other drunks works.

Take a look around at the next A.A. meeting you go to.
You will see smiling, healthy faces. Each A.A. member who
follows the program is as great a healing miracle as any re-
corded in the Bible. The age of miracles is alive and well in
A.A.!

On Last Resorts

If all else fails, don't drink!

If you can avoid drinking, you have a chance to learn
A.A.'s way of life; if you drink, you never will. Therefore, as
my sponsors said so often, "If all else fails, don't drink!"

Another hard-nose, who is a trial attorney, told me that in
court when his adversary "got his goat," that meant the adversary was winning. Alcohol is my adversary, and if I let
anything in my life get my goat to the extent that I drink
again, my adversary has won and I have lost.

On the Ultimate Answer

Shut up, don't drink, and go to meetings!

There was a period when I hated my sponsors. Of all the remarks they made to me, none upset me so much as this one. It didn't seem to matter what I asked or said to them — whether I complained of constipation, my boss, sore feet, or the latest things my kids had done — their reply was always the same: "Shut up, don't drink, and go to meetings!"

Then I figured it out. If all of the A.A. literature were somehow destroyed in a catastrophe, I still could stay sober. All I had to do was to stop fighting it, not drink, and go to meetings. I finally saw my sponsors' cruel remark in its true colors — a definition of the A.A. program in one line. So I did what they said. I hadn't realized how well I had learned the lesson until I recently caught myself telling a newcomer: "Shut up, don't drink, and go to meetings!"

It works, and to A.A. that's the only test that matters.

More guidance for your journey...

A Program for You
A Guide to the Big Book's Design for Living
  Combine the study tools in this guide to *Alcoholics Anonymous* with the knowledge of your Twelve Step program sponsor to create a firm foundation for recovery. *A Program for You* effectively and interestingly looks at the original AA text and shows how valuable and applicable it still is for Twelve Steppers today. 180 pp.
Order No. 5122

Guidance on Our Journeys
Sponsorship
  by Edward C. Sellner, Ph.D.
  How should you choose a sponsor? What can you do to create a beneficial relationship with a sponsor? Edward Sellner defines what you should look for in a Twelve Step sponsor, and what to do to have the best relationship with a sponsor. Pamphlet, 24 pp.
Order No. 1298

Hazelden's Pocket Power Series
  Keep these pocket-sized pamphlets nearby for those moments when you need reinforcement for the changes you're making in recovery. Each 16-page pamphlet provides wise guidance on a specific topic.

Order No. 5366 Accepting Criticism   Order No. 5351 Letting Go
Order No. 1336 Honesty   Order No. 5449 Surrender
Order No. 5349 Prayer and Meditation
Order No. 1339 Just for Today

For price and order information, or a free catalog, please call our Telephone Representatives.

HAZELDEN

1-800-328-9000   **1-651-213-4000**   **1-651-257-1331**
(Toll Free, U.S., Canada,   (Outside the U.S.   (FAX)
and the Virgin Islands)   and Canada)   http://www.hazelden.org

Pleasant Valley Road • P.O. Box 176 • Center City, MN 55012-0176